my friend is struggling with . . .

Death
of a
Loved One

my friend is struggling with . . .

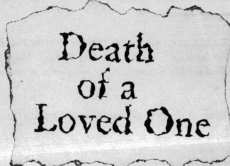

Death of a Loved One

Josh McDowell
& Ed Stewart

WORD PUBLISHING

NASHVILLE

A Thomas Nelson Company

Scripture quotations used in this book are from the Holy Bible, New International Version. Copyright © 1973, 1978, 1984, International Bible Society. Used by permission of Zondervan Bible Publishers.

Library of Congress Cataloging-in-Publication Data

McDowell, Josh.
    My friend is struggling with—death of a loved one / by Josh McDowell and Ed Stewart.
    p. cm.
    ISBN 0-8499-3791-4 (TP)
    1. Youth—Religious life. 2. Death—Religious aspects—Christianity. 3. Bereavement—Religious aspects—Christianity. 4. Grief—Religious aspects—Christianity. 5. Consolation. 6. Youth—Prayer books and devotions—English. I. Stewart, Ed. II. Title. III. Series.
    BV4905.2 .M313 2000
    248.8'66—dc21

00-024466
CIP

Printed in the United States of America

00 01 02 03 04 05 QDT 9 8 7 6 5 4 3 2 1

Acknowledgments

We would like to thank the following people:

David Ferguson, director of Intimate Life Ministries of Austin, Texas, has made a tremendous contribution to this collection. David's influence, along with the principles of the Intimate Life message, is felt throughout each book in this collection. David has modeled before us how to be God's comfort, support, and encouragement to others. We encourage you to take advantage of the seminars and resources that Intimate Life Ministries offers. (See pages 47–52 for more information about how this ministry can serve you.)

Dave Bellis, my (Josh) associate of twenty-three years, who labored with us to mold and

acknowledgments

shape each book in this collection. Each fictional story in all eight books of the PROJECT 911 collection was derived from the dramatic audio segments of the "Youth in Crisis Resource," which Dave personally wrote. He was also responsible for the design and coordination of the entire PROJECT 911 family of resources (see pages 55–58). We are so very grateful for Dave's talents and involvement.

Joey Paul of Word Publishing not only believed in this entire project, but also consistently championed it throughout Word.

JOSH MCDOWELL
ED STEWART

Chad's Story

It's Matty's fault, I just know it is," Chad Rogers hissed aloud to himself. It was dusk as the muscular sophomore marched along the dusty shoulder of the highway in a huff. Chad kicked at an occasional pebble, venting his anger toward his little brother. "He's not even seven years old yet, but Mom treats him like he's king of the world. She probably took him to the video store so the little brat could pick out another video game. No wonder she never got to the school to pick me up."

Chad's book bag was slung over one shoulder as he tramped along. The high school was half a mile behind him, and the Rogerses' country home was still three miles in the distance.

"I knew the plan wouldn't work," Chad mumbled to himself. "Mom should have been at the school more than an hour ago—*that* was the plan. She said she'd pick up Rob in town and be at school right after basketball practice. We have to eat supper by 5:30 so Rob and I can get to the church by 6:30. Now we won't have time to eat, and we may not even get to the church on time. If we aren't there, the youth group will go to the game without us. Matty is going to get it for this."

The country road was nearly deserted, as usual. But Chad heard a vehicle approaching in the distance behind him. It was probably Mom's van, he figured, but he wasn't about to turn around and look as if he were waiting for it. In fact, Chad decided he would just ignore the van when Mom stopped to pick him up. He would make Matty wait just as he had made him wait at the school. He would just keep walking. His friend Rob, who was coming with Mom and Matty, would understand. He had a bratty little brother too.

The vehicle slowed behind Chad as he'd expected. But when it pulled alongside him, it wasn't Mom's dark green van after all. From the corner of his eye Chad recognized his dad's pickup truck. "Chad," he called through the open window. Ben Rogers was a supervisor at the local cannery. He had been working ten- to twelve-hour shifts since the middle of summer.

Surprised to see his dad, Chad stopped and turned. "You're off work kind of early—"

He interrupted. "Chad, get in. Hurry."

Chad heard something in his voice he had never heard before. Dad wasn't angry at him, but he wasn't happy either. He sounded worried, kind of stressed out. *Maybe Mom panicked when she didn't find me at the school,* he thought, *so she called Dad to come look for me.*

Climbing into the truck, he started to explain. But Dad cut him off. Putting his hand on his shoulder, he said, "Chad, there's been . . . a very bad . . . accident." He was having trouble getting the words out. "We have to get to the hospital . . . right away."

An electric shock of fear shot through Chad. He gripped his dad's arm. "Mom? Matty? Are they all right?"

Ben's chin began to tremble and his eyes glistened with tears. "It's very bad, son. They all went to the hospital in an ambulance—Mom, Matthew, and Rob too." His voice cracked as he went on. "A big truck crossed the center line—"

"Dad, no!" Chad wailed, reading the agony in his face. "Not Mom, not Matty, not Rob! You're wrong. They're just late coming to pick me up." He turned to look out the back window, hoping to see the van pulling up. The road behind them was deserted.

"Chad, this is a terrible thing, but we have to hold it together and get to the hospital. Mom and Matthew need us now, and Rob needs you too."

Chad buried his face in his hands. "This can't happen," he said, fighting back the emotions. Then he thought of his older sister, who was away at college. "Does Beth know yet? Did you call her?"

"I came straight from work to find you, son. I'll call Beth when we get to the hospital and find out how Mom and Matty are doing."

Chad screamed in near hysteria. "Hurry, Dad, hurry!"

Ben put the truck in gear, turned it around, and raced back toward town. Feeling his dad's strong, assuring grip on his arm again, Chad heard him lift a simple prayer in a broken voice, "Help us, Father. Help our family. We need You now."

Please, God, help us, Chad echoed inside.

Arriving at the emergency room, they learned that Chad's six-year-old brother, Matthew, had died instantly when the produce truck had swerved across the line and hit the Rogerses' van head on. Chad, Ben, and several other family members sobbed in each other's arms. They were surrounded by a few shocked, grieving neighbors and friends who had raced to the hospital when they heard the news. Also in the circle was Pastor O'Neill from the church that Chad and his family attended.

The hospital's main waiting room was also filling with grieving friends. The youth group's trip to the high-school football game was canceled when news of the horrible crash reached the church. Several of Chad's and Rob's friends were in the waiting room consoling each other and praying for the two families. Doug and Jenny Shaw, the youth-group sponsors, were with them.

Chad's emotions took a beating during the first hour at the hospital. The numbing shock of Matty's death was followed by the painful reality that his critically injured mother and friend were still fighting for their lives. The group moved from the emergency room to the surgery waiting room to await news from the surgeons. Each new arrival of relatives to the hospital brought another wave of sorrow and tears. Chad's eyes were red and puffy, and his chest hurt. He could hardly keep his hands from shaking.

Encircled by relatives, Chad had failed to notice that Doug and Jenny Shaw had also come to the surgery waiting room. When they approached Chad and embraced him, Chad broke down again. The three of them stood crying together for a couple of minutes. The Shaws, who operated a small quick-print store in town, worked with the church youth group as volunteers. Doug led most of the youth Bible studies, and Jenny planned the activities. Doug and Jenny liked to joke that Chad was their adopted son.

Next to his own family, Chad could not think of anyone he loved more as "second parents."

The couple led Chad to a small sofa in the corner of the waiting room. Doug handed Chad a small bottle of cold juice he had bought from a vending machine down the hall. Chad thanked him and took a long drink.

"I can't believe what's happening to me," Chad said, fighting back tears.

"I know it hurts a lot, Chad." Doug's voice cracked with emotion. "And we really hurt for you."

"We love you, Chad," Jenny added, "and we wish you didn't have to go through this pain. We're so sorry about Matthew."

"Matty is gone, Mom and Rob are hurt badly, and I can't get control of my emotions," Chad lamented.

Doug patted Chad's arm. "It's okay. Go ahead and let it all out. We're here to cry with you and your family."

"I know God feels your hurt too, Chad," Jenny said. "If Jesus were here in the flesh right now, I think He would be crying too."

Chad sat silently for more than a minute, occasionally wiping a tear from his face. Doug and Jenny quietly kept him company, assuring him with gentle touches. Across the room, Pastor O'Neill and a few friends from church consoled and comforted Ben Rogers. Rob's family was also in the room, huddled with their loved ones. Everyone prayed that the grief they felt over Matthew's death would not be compounded by the loss of his mother, Margaret, or Chad's friend Rob, both of whom were still in emergency surgery.

"I feel awful about Matty, because I was mad at him," Chad said at last, shaking his head slightly. "I thought he was the reason Mom was late picking me up."

"I know that hurts," Doug consoled gently.

"I blamed my little brother for something he didn't do," Chad lamented. "It wasn't his fault. Matty died, and I didn't have a chance to apologize for being mad at him."

"We are so sorry you have to deal with those feelings, Chad," Jenny said. "We're going to be with you through this."

After several more silent seconds, Chad said, "Mom can't die; she just can't. She's my mom—we're really close, and I need her. Beth needs her too. God wouldn't take my mom away, would He? And Rob . . . why did this have to happen to my mom, my best friend, and my little brother? I don't think God is being fair."

Jenny gave Chad another gentle squeeze around the shoulder. "I'm so sad for you," she said with a quavering voice. "Seeing you hurt makes me hurt."

"I know there are family members who want to be with you," Doug said, "but we want to pray for you first, okay?"

Chad nodded meekly.

The three huddled closely together and linked hands as Doug began. "Heavenly Father, thank You for loving Chad and knowing all about his deep pain. Thank You for being here with us right now and sharing Your comfort through others. We ache inside at the loss of little Matthew, and we pray for Your divine intervention for Margaret and Rob in surgery at this moment. Rest Your hand of care and blessing on

Chad and his family as they deal with this tragedy. In Jesus' name we pray. Amen."

Chad looked up to see that his mother's older brother and his teenage boys had just arrived from their home two hours away. "I need to go see my uncle and cousins," he explained as he and the Shaws stood up.

"Of course, you go on," Doug said. "We'll stay around just to be here with you, okay?"

"I'd like that. Thanks." Then Chad hugged each of them and left to join his family.

Waiting for the doctors to come out of surgery was torture. In the meantime, Ben Rogers's attention was torn between the sad task of arranging for his little boy's body to be picked up by the funeral home and the frail hope that his wife would survive her massive injuries. Chad and Ben both talked to Beth on the phone. His older sister said she would get on a flight for home tonight. Chad was surprised at how calm she sounded on the phone.

Then, along with a room full of family and caring friends, they returned to waiting. People occasionally said things to Chad, apparently trying to cheer him up: "God must need your little brother in heaven more than we do"; "At least Matthew didn't suffer long"; "You should be thankful that God let you have him for six years"; "Everything will be all right." Chad knew the people meant well, but some of their comments did not make him feel any better. He found himself returning to Doug and Jenny occasionally just to hear them say "We're sorry" and "We're here for you."

Rob's surgeon came out first, and Chad held his breath as he began his report to family and friends. The gruesome details of his friend's life-threatening injuries and surgery made Chad shudder with shock and fear. Rob would be in intensive care for several days. He was on life support and had a fifty/fifty chance for survival. Chad joined Doug and Jenny to pray with Rob's parents.

When the second doctor, a neurosurgeon, walked into the waiting room about twenty minutes later, Chad wanted to run away and hide. If he didn't hear what the doctor said, he might be able to convince himself that his mom was fine, that this hospital nightmare was only about Matty and Rob. But Ben motioned Chad to his side on the sofa and draped a comforting arm around his shoulders. Then Chad placed his hand on Doug's arm.

The doctor sat on the coffee table and addressed Ben Rogers. "Your wife is out of surgery and holding her own for the moment. But I'm afraid the prognosis is not good. She suffered serious head trauma in the crash, and we did everything we could for her. But she is not breathing on her own and—I'm sorry to say—her brain activity is very weak."

"You mean my mom is brain dead?" The timid words tumbled out before Chad could stop them. He had studied a little about brain function in health class during spring term. At the time, "brain dead" seemed so unrelated to his personal life that the words could have been in a foreign language. Now they were horrifyingly real.

The surgeon turned to him. "We're going to monitor your mother's condition closely through the night, so we will have a better idea what we are facing in the morning. I'm not ready to say she is brain dead. But it doesn't look good. We have done all we can medically, but I also believe in prayer and miracles. The rest is up to the Great Physician."

Chad squeezed his eyes closed to shut out the cruel world assaulting him. Had his father and Doug not been surrounding him at the moment, he might have bolted from the room.

"When can we see her?" Ben asked the doctor, his voice breaking.

"She should be in ICU by now," the doctor said, standing. "She is in a deep coma, but hearing your voices may be a comfort to her. A few of you may go back if you like."

Chad knew he had to go see his mother, but he hesitated at the idea. To Chad, walking through those doors meant that his mother was really in a hospital room connected to machines to stay alive, and he did not want to admit that. Horrible accidents occurred in other people's lives, not in his. Moments later Chad found himself walking with Doug Shaw down a dimly lit hall toward ICU. Pastor O'Neill and Ben Rogers walked ahead. Jenny had left after volunteering to pick up Beth at the airport and bring her to the hospital.

When Chad first glimpsed the patient on the bed, he felt relieved. It was not his mother. At least it did not look like his mother. The woman's puffy face was a collage of dark blue, purple, crimson, and pasty white. Her head was swathed in a bandage from the surgery. Tubes protruding from her mouth and nose further distorted her face. And her eyes were covered by swollen, bluish-purple lids; they weren't the sparkling green eyes that Chad knew. Chad moved closer to confirm the faint hope that this was someone else's mother, not his.

But his dad's reaction told Chad the truth. He slipped his hand around his wife's pale, limp hand on the sheet and began talking to her softly, lovingly. After a minute, it was Chad's turn. He moved to the bed to stand beside his father.

Gazing upon the still form, Chad could finally see a resemblance. The shock of hair sticking out of the bandage was his mother's color. The shape of her ear and dimpled chin were also familiar. *I don't want it to be you, Mom, but it is you,* he admitted silently.

At this moment Chad shed no tears. Another strong emotion was boiling up inside him as he gazed on the near-lifeless body. Chad clenched his jaw to keep the sudden, angry words from blurting out of his mouth: *God, why did You let this happen to my mother?*

Time Out to Consider

As Chad has discovered, it is incredibly painful and difficult to cope with the death of a loved one or close friend. You may have made that same discovery. Whether it is a parent or grandparent succumbing to terminal cancer, a friend or classmate killed in a car accident, a baby brother or sister who just goes to sleep and never wakes up, or any loss of someone dear to you, it hurts. Death seems especially painful and difficult to accept when it is sudden and unexpected, like the crash that killed Matthew Rogers or a fatal heart attack or a brutal act of violence.

There are a couple of things to notice from

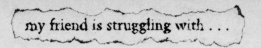

the first part of Chad's story that may be helpful as you face the sadness of a loved one's death.

First, you may experience a wide range of emotions when someone close to you dies. Like Chad, you may feel terribly sad, depressed, hopeless, abandoned, frightened, and even angry because of what happened. You may cry as you have never cried in your life. You may feel emotionally drained and exhausted. And you may get intensely angry at the situation, at the person who died and left you alone, at the person(s) you consider responsible for the death, or even at God for allowing it to happen. It is important to understand that all these feelings are normal and natural. It is the way God wired you. Your emotions are a built-in release valve to help you handle deep inner pain. Of course, there are both productive and unproductive ways of expressing these emotions.

Doug and Jenny's simple advice to Chad in the waiting room was sound. They encouraged him not to bottle up his feelings, but to let his grief flow out. They said they were there to hurt with him and cry with him. This response reflects Jesus' words in Matthew 5:4: "Blessed are those who mourn, for they will be comforted." Mourning is the process of getting the hurt out. You share your hurt so others can share your pain and hurt with you so you are not alone. This is God's design for blessing you and beginning to heal the deep pain that accompanies a tragic loss. It is good and necessary to experience the different emotions that come at this time.

Second, your greatest need in the first hours after the death of a friend or loved one is for others to comfort you. That's why Doug and Jenny Shaw rushed to the hospital to be with Chad and his father. In a time of deep sorrow, our greatest comfort comes when others sorrow with us. One major way God shares His comfort with us is through other people. The apostle Paul wrote, "God . . . comforts us in all our troubles, so that we can comfort those in any trouble with the comfort we ourselves have received from God" (2 Cor. 1:3, 4).

What is comfort? Maybe it will help to see first what comfort is *not*. Comfort is not a "pep talk" urging you to hang in there, to tough it out, or to hold it together. Comfort is not an attempt to explain why things happen to people. Comfort is not a bunch of positive words about God being in control and everything being okay. All of these things may be good and useful in time, but they do not fill our primary need for comfort.

People comfort us primarily by feeling our hurt and sorrowing with us. Jesus illustrated the ministry of comfort when His friend Lazarus died (see John 11). When Jesus arrived at the home of Lazarus's sisters, Mary and Martha, He wept with them (see vv. 33–35). His response is especially interesting in light of what He did next: raise Lazarus from the dead (see vv. 38–44).

Why didn't Jesus simply tell the grieving Mary and Martha, "No need to cry, My friends, because in a few minutes Lazarus will be alive again"? Because at that moment they needed someone to identify with their loss. Jesus met Mary's and Martha's need for comfort by sharing in their sorrow and tears. Later He performed the miracle that turned their sorrow to joy.

We receive comfort when we know we are not suffering alone. Paul instructed us, "Rejoice with those who rejoice; mourn with those who mourn" (Rom. 12:15). When you experience sorrow, people may try to comfort you by cheering you up, urging you to be strong, or trying to explain away the tragic event. These people no doubt care about you and mean well by their words. But they may not know what comfort sounds like. Hopefully, there will also be someone around like Doug and Jenny Shaw who will provide the comfort you need. You will sense God's care and concern for you as this someone hurts with you, sorrows with you, and weeps with you. The Shaws are a good example of what real comfort looks like in a tragic and sorrowful circumstance.

But there is much more to getting through the death of a loved one, as Chad Rogers is yet to discover.

Chad's Story

Chad and his father practically lived at the hospital over the weekend, going home late at night only to sleep, shower, and change clothes. Family members, neighbors, and church friends were helpful and supportive. Neighbors took over the care of the Rogerses' two big dogs during the day. Friends brought meals and flowers to the hospital. And a number of people visited at the hospital as father and son stood vigil in the ICU. Chad most appreciated the timely visits of Doug and Jenny Shaw.

Chad slept only a few fitful hours on Friday and Saturday night. Awaking very early each morning, he prayed that the horrors of Friday evening were only a bad dream. He lay in bed for several anxious minutes, imagining that Mom, Dad, and Matty were waiting to eat breakfast with him in the kitchen. But when he found his dad alone in the kitchen each morning huddled over a cup of coffee and weeping, cold reality broke over him again.

On Sunday morning, Ben and Chad attended their church's early service before driving to the hospital. Soon after they arrived, Chad's best friend Rob died. Chad left his mother's bedside for a short while to grieve with Rob's parents, with Doug and Jenny, and with a group of kids from the youth group who had come to the hospital after church. Chad missed Rob terribly. He also confided to Doug that he felt a little responsible for Rob's death. "If I hadn't begged him to come with me Friday night, he wouldn't have been in the van." Doug's care and understanding were really helpful.

Sunday afternoon, with the help of Pastor O'Neill, Ben and Chad started talking about Matthew's funeral. But Ben decided to postpone the service until the doctors could give him a clearer prognosis for Margaret. Beth, Chad's older sister, refused to talk about the funeral. She spent a few hours at the hospital on Saturday, but she showed little emotion. She preferred to stay with her friends in town as her father and brother waited and prayed for Margaret to show any faint signs of recovery.

Monday morning, after consulting with the neurosurgeon, Ben approached his son in the ICU waiting room where he sat with Doug, who had stopped by on his way to work. Chad studied his father's face. It was shadowed with the grief they had both carried since Friday night.

Dad sat down beside his son and spoke softly with great sadness in his voice. "Chad, I have very sad news. Dr. Nordvall just told me that Mom is not going to come out of the coma. He consulted other brain specialists, and they all agree. She's not going to make it. It's only a matter of time."

Chad dropped his head as he choked back his emotion. "I don't know what to say, Dad," he said at last.

"That's all right, son," Ben assured him. "I'm going to find Beth and tell her the doctor's news. We can all get together later this morning."

After his dad left, Chad talked with Doug for a few minutes, and they shared a brief time of prayer. Doug left for work, promising that he would be back around noon to check on him.

Chad found himself alone in the room with his mother. He stared for several minutes at the still form on the bed as the respirator pumped life into her breath by breath. The large, dark bruises on her pasty white face were tinged with sickly yellow. The woman looked more like a stranger than like Chad's mom.

Leaning close to his mother's ear, Chad whispered, "I don't want you to die. I miss you already." Realizing there would be no response from Mom, Chad bowed his head. "Lord, I want You to perform a miracle and heal my mother. But if You choose not to do it, tell me now. I can't stand to see her this way." Feeling exhausted in every way, Chad leaned back in the chair and fell asleep.

Early that afternoon, the family invited Pastor O'Neill and close friends to gather around Margaret for prayer. Chad, however, declined the invitation. He waited outside with some others, staying close to Doug Shaw. "This really isn't happening, Doug, not to me."

"I know. It's unreal, like a bad nightmare."

"Mom can't die now; she just can't. She has to be here when I graduate and go off to college. We have so many plans. She just can't die. It isn't fair."

"I'm so sorry you won't have your mother to share in all of that, Chad," Doug consoled. "What else have you been feeling?"

Chad hesitated. "Sometimes I feel mad. Is that wrong?"

Doug patted the young man's shoulder.

23

"Anger is a common, normal reaction. Tell me about it."

"I'm mad at the other driver for letting his truck cross the center line. And why doesn't the county have wider roads? Maybe Mom could have swerved around the truck." Chad paused to wipe a small tear from his eye. "And I'm a little mad at God for letting this happen. He could have kept that truck from crossing the line. Why didn't He? The truck could have hit someone else's car, someone who didn't have any children."

Doug nodded. "It's hard to understand why it happened this way, isn't it?"

Doug paused, then he asked, "Anything else going on inside that you want to talk about?"

Chad looked away for a moment. Then he answered in a voice he hoped would not carry beyond them. "I think what happened to Mom and Matty may be partly my fault."

"Your fault? What do you mean?"

Chad dropped his head. "I haven't been very consistent in my devotions lately. If I had been praying for my family like I should, maybe Mom wouldn't have been in the crash."

"Oh Chad," Doug said, "I'm so sorry that you've been bothered by such a thought."

Chad went on. "Last night I confessed it to God. I told Him that I would be more faithful and obedient to Him if He would just let Mom live." At that moment, Ben and Pastor O'Neill pushed through the door and slowly entered the room. Chad looked up, sensing the news in his father's face. "But I guess my prayer was too late."

There were only a few tears as Ben reported to those assembled in the room, "Margaret is with the Lord now—and with Matthew." As family members and close friends embraced each other and left the hospital in twos and threes, they seemed relieved and grateful that Margaret's brief suffering was over. But her fifteen-year-old son was still struggling with a storm of conflicting feelings.

Before leaving the hospital, Doug took Chad aside for one last comment. "None of this is your fault, Chad," he whispered with compassion in his gaze. "But don't worry. I'll be here to help you get through it."

Time Out to Consider

It has been less than three days since the tragic accident that rocked Chad Rogers's world, but he is already starting the common process most people go through after such a sad event. The grieving process, which may continue for several weeks or months, has five clearly identifiable stages. No two people go through the process in exactly the same way, and the stages often overlap and recur. But you will likely find yourself responding to your personal tragedy something like Chad did.

One of the first responses to grief is *denial*. You may find yourself at times unwilling to believe that such a terrible thing is happening to you. Chad displayed this response when he resisted going into his mother's room at the hospital. He did not want to see his injured mother at first because it would confirm that the accident had really happened. Later he tried to convince himself that it was all a bad dream. One of the ways your mind and emotions will try to handle the shock of your grief is to say, "No way; this is not happening to me."

26

A second stage in responding to grief is *anger*. When grappling with the inevitable question—"Why did this happen?"—you may find yourself lashing out angrily because there is no reasonable answer to that question. You have lost someone very dear to you, and it seems terribly unfair. Like Chad, your anger may be directed in a number of different ways. You may be angry at the cause of death (the car, the highway department, the cancer, the heart attack, etc.). You may feel anger toward person(s) you think are at least partially to blame (the other driver, the doctor, the perpetrator of the crime, etc.). Strange as it seems, you may be angry at the person who died ("Why did you leave me alone?") or at God for allowing it to happen. Your anger may even be directed at yourself because you suspect that you were somehow to blame for what happened. Chad experienced each of these levels of anger.

A third stage of grief is *bargaining* with God for relief from the awful event and its consequences. You may find yourself secretly trying to cut a deal with God as Chad did, vowing to change your behavior if He will bring back your loved one or make the pain or the reality of separation go away. Chad's plea to God was motivated by his sense of false guilt over not being a better Christian, which he feared had caused the tragedy in some way. You may be prompted to try to cut a deal with God both to change the circumstance and make up for perceived failures.

Another stage of grief is *depression,* which comes when you realize that your loved one is really gone. It's the feeling of overwhelming sadness or hopelessness over the loss. Depression may be accompanied by fear, anxiety, or insecurity about living on without your loved one. Intense loneliness is another facet of depression. Sitting beside his comatose mother, Chad expressed how much he already missed her and how disappointed he was that his mom would not be there for him in the years ahead.

The final stage of grief is *acceptance.* As time goes by and the other stages of grief diminish, you will be able to accept the reality of your loss and begin to deal with it constructively. Even as this stage becomes dominant, you may still experience pangs of denial, anger, and depression. But they will be minimal compared to the more positive sense that God is working out your experience for good (see Rom. 8:28).

Christian counselors and leaders generally agree that it is normal and healthy to experience the five stages of grief following the death of a loved one. In many cases it takes many weeks or months to navigate successfully all five stages. Some of the emotions and thoughts that you experience during this time may be new to you or stronger than ever before in your life. You may wonder if there is something wrong with you for reacting in these ways. There is not. You are going through a common response to a very sad event in your life.

The only real danger as you move through these stages is allowing yourself to express your feelings in inappropriate or unhealthy ways. For example, if Chad's anger tempted him to seek revenge against the driver of the truck or if his depression caused him to attempt suicide, he would be responding to his grief in an improper and unhealthy way. It is wise not to respond impulsively to any of the strong emotions you encounter as you move through the stages of grief.

One of your best allies in dealing with the death of a loved one is time. The old proverb "Time heals all wounds" contains a nugget of truth. Accept the fact that it will take time for you to get over your great loss. You need time to process the jumble of feelings and thoughts. You need time to talk out your feelings with mature, compassionate Christian friends and leaders. As the weeks pass, your sorrow will diminish and your life will return to a fairly normal pattern. Give time a chance to work for you by not expecting the pain and confusion to go away too soon.

Now that his mother is gone, Chad is just beginning a new phase in his journey of grief. Thankfully, he does not have to make this journey alone.

Chad's Story

The memorial service for Margaret and Matthew Rogers was scheduled for Friday morning at the church. With his father's encouragement, Chad elected to stay home from school for the week. It gave him time to grieve with Dad and Beth and other relatives, many of whom had come from out of state.

Chad was amazed at the practical support supplied by friends and church members like Doug and Jenny Shaw. He had expressed concern to Doug that he might fall behind on his schoolwork during his week away. So Doug went to the school, contacted each of Chad's teachers, and collected assignments he could do at home. He just saw the need and filled it. Chad found it helpful to divert his concentration to homework a couple of hours each day.

Pastor O'Neill told Ben and Chad and Beth not to worry about fixing meals for themselves. Every evening, a different church family showed up at the house with a delicious covered-dish supper, plenty of food for the Rogerses and Chad's uncle and his family, who were staying with them for the week. Church families and friends in town volunteered to house other visiting relatives. And someone was always available to run errands and help with household chores. Doug and Jenny Shaw were right in the middle of making sure Chad and his family were cared for in practical ways.

In addition to the support, Chad felt overwhelmed at the encouragement people shared with him and his family. Several bouquets and potted plants were delivered to the house every day. Scores of cards and letters arriving by mail were filled with kind words of concern and love. Many people called to share their love and sympathy and ask how the family was doing. Chad was especially blessed by the oversize card sent to him by the members of the church youth group. Everyone had written in it, signed it, and included a Scripture verse.

Even with all the support and encouragement, Chad had his down times. "I really get emotional around bedtime," he confided in Doug Thursday evening. "Mom usually came in to chat and pray with me before I turned out the light. I miss that so much already." Chad and Doug were sipping blended fruit smoothies at the local health-food shop. Doug had invited him out just to ask how he was doing. Chad realized it felt good to be out of the house for a little while.

"I feel so sad that you won't have that nightly visit with your mom, Chad," Doug consoled.

Chad sipped his drink and continued, "I seem to cycle through those different feelings you talked to me about. Mostly I'm either very sad or very mad—and either way, I get really emotional."

"That's okay, Chad," Doug said. "It's part of the process."

"I'm worried about Beth though," Chad said with a little frown. "She hasn't cried once, and she doesn't want to talk about what happened to Mom or Matty. She spends most of the day with her friends or in her room alone. Is there anything I can do for her?"

"Two things come to mind," Doug answered. "First, comfort her as best you can. Think of the special times she enjoyed with your mother and—"

"Beth and Mom kept in touch on the computer," Chad interrupted. "They exchanged e-mail several times a week."

"Okay, maybe you could say to her, 'Beth, I'm sorry that you won't be able to chat with Mom by e-mail anymore. I know that was very special to you.'"

"Just like you comforted me about missing my nightly visits with Mom."

"Exactly," Doug said with a wink. "And if you think of other specific areas where she is hurting about the loss of your mother and brother, you can offer words of comfort there too."

"I can do that," Chad agreed, "because I'm sure Beth and I are struggling in some of the same areas about Mom and Matty."

"The second thing you can do is pray for her," Doug said. "Ask God to help her receive the comfort she needs. That's what Jenny and I have been praying for. And we're praying for you too, Chad, every day."

Chad poked at the frothy drink with his straw. "Thank you," he said meekly. "It means a lot that you check up on me. And thanks for the nice card you and Jenny sent. Dad and I have been real close this week, but it's great to know that you are here too."

Doug nodded. "That's what it's all about to be in a family of believers, isn't it?"

Chad smiled and agreed.

Chad woke up the next morning dreading the funeral, expecting it to be sad, somber, and depressing. But he was wrong. There were many tears in the crowded sanctuary, especially in the rows where Chad sat with his family. But Pastor O'Neill conducted the service as a praise to God for the lives of his mother and brother. The songs sung and words spoken assured Chad that God is good and gracious when tragedy strikes. Even the brief service at the cemetery had an uplifting note as Pastor O'Neill reminded the family of the resurrection to come at Christ's appearing.

After the services, the church hosted a potluck supper in the fellowship hall for all who wanted to attend. Chad was surrounded by a crowd of loving people for a couple of hours. But as the people began to leave, he felt a little anxious. By tomorrow most of his visiting family would be gone, and on Sunday, Beth would fly back to college. Chad and his father would be alone for the first time since Margaret and

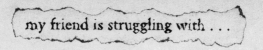
Matthew died. And Chad was not sure how he
would handle it.

Time Out to Consider

Chad needed more than the comfort of his family and loving friends to get through his terrible
loss, and so do you. There are two more important elements that hopefully are being supplied
to you.

First, *you need the support of others.* What's
the difference between comfort and support?
People supply the comfort you need when they
share your sorrow emotionally. People supply the
support you need by helping you during this
time in practical ways. The day-to-day tasks of
life go on even after a tragedy. But you may have
little attention or energy for such things because
you are dealing with such a heavy emotional bur-
den. You and others in your family need tempo-
rary help just to get these things done. You need
the help of people who are committed to obeying
Galatians 6:2: "Carry each other's burdens, and
in this way you will fulfill the law of Christ."

Think about the ways Chad and his family were supported by others. Doug helped by picking up Chad's schoolwork and bringing it to him. Church families helped by preparing and delivering meals, running errands, and providing housing for visiting family members. And an even larger number of people showed their support by attending the memorial service. Whenever something needed to be done, someone was ready to do it for them. People made themselves available to carry these daily burdens for the Rogerses while their energies were focused on their grief.

You may be tempted to ignore or to refuse the support offered by others. You may feel that you can handle it yourself, or you may not want others to be bothered with things you normally do for yourself. Resist that temptation. God put Galatians 6:2 in the Bible because He knows there are times we should rely on the support of others. This is such a time. Let other people do things for you, and be grateful for their help. It is one of the ways God is providing for your needs at this time.

What if you have a need and nobody steps up

to offer help? Ask for it. There is nothing wrong with telling a trusted friend, a youth leader, or your minister about your need and asking for help. For example, had Doug not thought about picking up Chad's schoolwork, Chad could have asked him to help in that way. In most cases, people are more than willing to help out; they just don't know what needs to be done. Feel free to help people support you at this time by letting them know what you need.

Second, *you need the encouragement of others.* You receive encouragement when someone does something thoughtful to lift your spirits. Chad was encouraged whenever Doug called or stopped by just to see how he was doing. He was encouraged by the flowers that came from so many people. He was encouraged by each hug from a family member or friend. He was encouraged by the card sent by the youth group, especially the personal comments and Scripture verses each member wrote. Encouraging deeds like these may not seem as practical as providing meals and running errands, but they are just as necessary.

Once again, if you do not receive the encouragement you need, ask for it. It's okay to tell someone who cares about you, "I need a hug" or "I just need you to be with me for a while."

Since it will take time for you to move through the stages of grief after your loss, you will continue to need comfort, support, and encouragement for some time. Your needs will not be as great as they were at first, but don't assume that you will be ready to resume life as usual right after the funeral. As Chad discovered in the month following the memorial service, you must allow your friends and family to continue their ministry of caring as long as you need it.

Chad's Story

Doug picked Chad up at 9:30 Saturday morning. They had not gone to the driving range since before Chad's mom and brother died just over a month earlier. Doug had been away at a business conference all week, so the first thing he asked as they drove away was, "How are you doing, Chad?"

Chad knew he would ask because he usually did. "I'm doing pretty okay. I still miss Mom a lot, and I have my emotional moments, but I know it's part of the process. I'm so glad you told me about the different stages of grief. If I didn't know they were part of the process, I might think there was something wrong with me for feeling angry or trying to bargain with God at times."

Chad shared a little more about his week, then Doug asked. "How about Beth? Is she doing all right?"

Chad sighed. "It's hard to tell because she's away at school. She calls about once a week, but she doesn't talk about Mom or Matty or the accident. I have been praying for her, and I've tried to comfort her like you suggested. But I think she is still hurting and doesn't know how to deal with it."

Doug nodded. "Some people have a difficult time dealing with their pain and receiving comfort. Just keep praying for her and looking for ways to share comfort. Jenny and I will do the same."

"Thanks."

Doug turned onto the main highway leading to the driving range, then he asked, "What has been the greatest help to you in getting through your times of denial, anger, and depression this month?"

Chad thought for a moment. "Two things. The first is hope. I'm really confident that I will see Mom and Matty and Rob again in heaven some day. I have heard the Bible verses about heaven since I was a small child. But in the last few weeks, that truth has really become real to me. I don't know how people make it without the hope of being with Christ and seeing their loved ones again.

"The second thing is having people like you to be with. My close friends at church have been great about spending time with me when I'm missing Rob. And if I need to talk, some of them are willing to listen to me, just like you do. It has brought us all closer together."

"That's what happens when friends really comfort one another like the Bible says," Doug interjected.

"And Dad has been great. Some days he will

sit down with me and ask what I'm thinking. At other times we don't even have to talk. We just hug—and sometimes we even cry. I don't know how, but being together and crying together seem to ease the pain of losing Mom and Matty. We are closer than we have ever been."

"That's wonderful, Chad."

"And do you know what is happening? Sometimes I can think about Mom and Matty and Rob and enjoy the good memories without the pain getting in the way. I still miss them a lot, but I'm also very thankful for the time I had with each of them. I'm sure that the hope I feel and the comfort of others—plus time—will eventually heal even my deepest hurts."

"I'm happy to hear that for at least two reasons," Doug said. "One, I'm just happy for how God is helping you through this very difficult time. Two, I want to talk to you about Marty Keller."

"Marty Keller? He's the new freshman in our youth group, right?"

"Right," Doug said. "Marty and his family started attending our church about a month ago."

Chad shrugged. "I don't really know him very well yet."

"Neither do I," Doug said. "But Pastor O'Neill called this morning to tell us that Marty's grandfather died suddenly of a stroke yesterday. Marty was very close to his grandparents, and he is really hurting."

"Oh, no," Chad said. "I'll bet Marty could use some comfort right now."

"That's what I thought," Doug agreed. Then he was silent.

It didn't take Chad long to take the hint. He turned to Doug and smiled. "Maybe we could stop by Marty's house on the way to the driving range—just for a couple of minutes. I have some comfort I could share with him."

Doug smiled back. "That sounds a lot like Second Corinthians chapter one, verses three and four where Paul talks about comforting others as God has comforted us through others."

"Just what I was thinking," Chad said. "Let's go on a mission of comfort."

"We're on our way," Doug said as he turned the car in the direction of the Keller home.

Time Out to Consider

Chad Rogers has been through a very tough experience in the last month. Losing his mother, brother, and best friend in the space of only a few days was a painful emotional blow. But he is getting through it. He is rejoicing in the hope of seeing them again in heaven. He is able to start enjoying the good memories without deep feelings of pain. And he is even able to empathize and share comfort with someone else. Chad has not finished the grieving process yet, but he is making great progress.

The pain of your loss may be so great right now that you wonder if you will ever get back to normal. Keep these keys in mind as you trust God to get you through this sad experience.

Let your sorrow be expressed. God designed your emotions to help you vent the pain of your loss. Don't stuff your feelings of sorrow inside; let them out so your heart can start healing.

Allow others to comfort you, support you, and encourage you. God's design for healing your grief includes using other people. Let loving family members and friends cry with you and care for you in practical ways.

Give yourself time to grieve. Moving through the stages of grief—denial, anger, bargaining, depression, and acceptance—may take many weeks or months. Be assured that, as time passes, things will get better.

Hold on to the hope of God's goodness. If your loved one was a Christian, you will see him or her in heaven again some day. If you are not sure about his or her faith, be assured that God is loving and just, and He always does what is right.

Allow God to use you to comfort, support, and encourage others. Your experience of receiving comfort from others has uniquely equipped you to help others in sorrow. It may take time, but you will have an opportunity to pass along comfort, support, and encouragement to someone who has lost a family member or friend.

APPENDIX

MORE ABOUT INTIMATE
LIFE MINISTRIES

Several times in this book I have mentioned the work of Dr. David Ferguson. David's ministry has had such a profound effect on me in the past several years that I want you to have every opportunity to be exposed to his work and ministry. David and his wife, Teresa, direct a ministry called Intimate Life Ministries.

WHO AND WHAT IS INTIMATE LIFE MINISTRIES?
Intimate Life Ministries (ILM) is a training and resource ministry whose purpose is to *assist in the development of Great Commandment ministries worldwide.* Great Commandment ministries—ministries that help us love God and our neighbors—are ongoing ministries that deepen

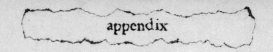

our intimacy with God and with others in marriage, family, and the church.

Intimate Life Ministries comprises:

- A network of **churches** seeking to fortify homes and communities with God's love;

- A network of **pastors and other ministry leaders** walking intimately with God and their families and seeking to live vulnerably before their people;

- A team of **accredited trainers** committed to helping churches establish ongoing Great Commandment ministries;

- A team of **professional associates** from ministry and other professional Christian backgrounds, assisting with research, training, and resource development;

- **Christian broadcasters, publishers, media, and other affiliates,** cooperating to see marriages and families reclaimed as divine relationships;

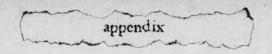

- **Headquarters staff** providing strategic planning, coordination, and support.

How Can Intimate Life Ministries Serve You?
ILM's Intimate Life Network of Churches is an effective, ongoing support and equipping relationship with churches and Christian leaders. There are at least four ways ILM can serve you:

1. *Ministering to Ministry Leaders*
ILM offers a unique two-day "Galatians 6:6" retreat to ministers and their spouses for personal renewal and for reestablishing and affirming ministry and family priorities. The conference accommodations and meals are provided as a gift to ministry leaders by cosponsoring partners. Thirty to forty such retreats are held throughout the U.S. and Europe each year.

2. *Partnering with Denominations and Other Ministries*
Numerous denominations and ministries have partnered with ILM by "commissioning" them to equip their ministry leaders through the Galatians

6:6 retreats along with strategic training and ongoing resources. This unique partnership enables a denomination to use the expertise of ILM trainers and resources to perpetuate a movement of Great Commandment ministry at the local level. ILM also provides a crisis-support setting to which denominations may send ministers, couples, or families who are struggling in their relationships.

3. *Identifying, Training, and Equipping Lay Leaders*

ILM is committed to helping the church equip its lay leaders through:

- *Sermon Series* on several Great Commandment topics to help pastors communicate a vision for Great Commandment health as well as identify and cultivate a core lay leadership group.

- *Community Training Classes* that provide weekly or weekend training to church staff and lay leaders. Classes are delivered by Intimate

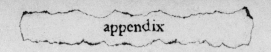

Life trainers along with ILM video-assisted training, workbooks, and study courses.

- *One-Day Training Conferences* on implementing Great Commandment ministry in the local church through marriage, parenting, or singles ministry. Conducted by Intimate Life trainers, these conferences are a great way to jump-start Great Commandment ministry in a local church.

4. *Providing Advanced Training and Crisis Support*

ILM conducts advanced training for both ministry staff and lay leaders through the Leadership Institute, focusing on relational ministry (marriage, parenting, families, singles, men, women, blended families, and counseling). The Enrichment Center provides support to relationships in crisis through Intensive Retreats for couples, families, and singles.

For more information on how you, your church, or your denomination can take advantage of the many services and resources, such as the Great Commandment Ministry Training Resource offered by Intimate Life Ministries, write or call:

Intimate Life Ministries
P.O. Box 201808
Austin, TX 78720-1808
1-800-881-8008
www.ilmministries.com

Connecting Youth in Crisis

Obtain other vital topics from the PROJECT 911 Collection...

Experience the Connection

JOSH McDOWELL'S PROJECT 911

For Youth & Youth Groups

This eight-week youth group experience will teach your youth the true meaning of deepened friendships—being a 911 friend. Each lesson is built upon scriptural teachings that will both bond your group together and serve to draw others to Christ.

This optional video is an excellent supplement to your group's workbook experience.

As follow-up to your youth group experience, continue a young person's friendship journey by introducing them to a thirty-day topical devotional journal and a book on discovering God's will in their life.

Experience the Connection

For Adults & Groups

This watershed book is for parents, pastors, youth workers, or anyone interested in seeing youth not only survive but thrive in today's culture.

Book on Audio

This book, directed specifically to fathers, offers ten qualities to form deepened relationships between dads and their kids.

Begin your church-wide emphasis with an adult group experience using this five-part video series. Josh provides biblical insights for relationally connecting with your youth.

Experience the Connection

JOSH McDOWELL'S PROJECT 911

For Youth Workers

A one-on-one resource to help you provide a relational response and spiritual guidance to the 24 most troubling issues youth face today.

This handbook brings together over forty youth specialists to share their insights on what makes a successful youth ministry.

Contact your Christian supplier to obtain these PROJECT 911 resources and begin experiencing the connection God intended.

ABOUT THE AUTHORS

JOSH MCDOWELL, internationally known speaker, author and traveling representative of Campus Crusade for Christ, International, has authored or coauthored more than fifty books, including *Right from Wrong* and *Josh McDowell's Handbook on Counseling Youth*. Josh and his wife, Dottie, have four children and live in Dallas, Texas.

ED STEWART is the author or coauthor of numerous Christian books. A veteran writer, Ed Stewart began writing fiction for youth as a coauthor with Josh McDowell. He has since authored four suspense novels for adults. Ed and his wife, Carol, live in Hillsboro, Oregon. They have two grown children and four grandchildren.